Literature written for young adults...

by young adults.

Allow yourself to be surprised.

Dinner at Tiffany's

Young Writers Chapbook Series

Mariah Cooper

Press

Atlanta

Copyright © 2013 by Mariah Cooper
Published by VerbalEyze Press

All rights reserved. Printed in the United States of America. No part of this book may be used or reproduced in any manner whatsoever, including Internet usage, without written permission from VerbalEyze Press except in the case of brief quotations embodied in critical articles and reviews.

Cover art © 2013 by Susan Arauz Barnes
Editing by Derek Koehl and Tavares Stephens
ISBN: 978-0-9856451-8-2

VerbalEyze Press books are available at special discounts for bulk purchases in the United States by corporations, institutions and other organizations.

For information, address VerbalEyze Press, 1376 Fairbanks Street SW, Atlanta, Georgia 30310.

VerbalEyze does not participate, endorse, or have any authority or responsibility concerning private correspondence between our authors and the public. All mail addressed to authors are forwarded, but the publisher cannot, unless specifically instructed by the author, give out an address or phone number.

VerbalEyze Press
A division of VerbalEyze, Inc.
www.verbaleyze.org

I dedicate this to my imagination.

Table of Contents

Foreword 11
Editors' Note 13
Dinner with Audrey Hepburn 15
The Old Me 17
Leaving Life Lonely 19
MA 21
13 Ways of Looking at a Picture 23
The Eye of the Beholder 29
Happy Ended 33
Slave 37
From the Back of My Closet 41
A Poet 45
Burial Ground 47

Dinner at Tiffany's

Foreword

Many a black and white speckled notebook has been privy to the growing pains of young artists. They sketch, narrate, poet and rhyme to make sense of the world and orient themselves to the gravitational pull of coming of age. But their musings beg for answers and an empathetic head nod, so YaHeard? Poetics was born.

Whether speaking heartache at the mic, spitting social commentary over tracks or texting observations into the ether, the power and influence of word is undeniable and YaHeard? Poets study the craft, explore their creative process and learn how to promote their artistic endeavors through collaborations with organizations like VerbalEyze, a beacon for young artists.

YaHeard? was founded by Educator-Artists to support the creative stirrings of tweens and teens and the publication of this chapbook honors and encourages the work of a young artists whose passion and talent confirms them as part of a new generation of prolific writers, artists and musicians. Their musings have escaped from first notebooks and into your hands. Answer if you dare; head nod if you must ---this young scribe dares to explore the power of voice.

Ya Heard?

Susan Arauz Barnes
Co-founder, YaHeard? Poetics

Editors' Note

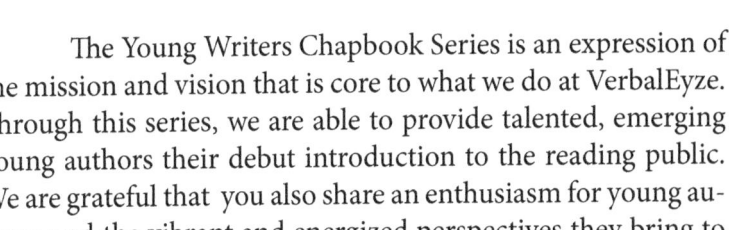

The Young Writers Chapbook Series is an expression of the mission and vision that is core to what we do at VerbalEyze. Through this series, we are able to provide talented, emerging young authors their debut introduction to the reading public. We are grateful that you also share an enthusiasm for young authors and the vibrant and energized perspectives they bring to our shared understanding of the human experience and what it means to live, love, long, lose and wonder as we travel together through this world.

We are pleased to bring to you an exceptional young writer, Mariah Cooper, with this edition of the Young Writers Chapbook. We trust that you will be as engaged and challenged by her words as we have been. Mariah is part of an exceptional group of young writers, YaHeard? Poetics. She and her fellow writers are an never-ending encouragement and inspiration to us.

Read, enjoy and, as always, *allow yourself to be surprised*.

Derek Koehl
Tavares Stephens

Dinner with Audrey Hepburn

this lonely dinner at tiffany's
black onyx with a side of sterling silver
this no dollar menu is killin me
a lonely dinner at tiffany's
where I belong to nobody
 nobody belongs to me
a country girl with
a no named cat
in the middle of New York City
The thoughts of what coulda been
what shoulda been
thoughts of what will never happen
this lonely dinner at Tiffany's
leaves me mourning
Breakfast

The Old Me

The old me

The old me was better

But now I sit alone writing love letters

 'Cause the old me

The old me

The old me was better

From daisy dukes to wearing house sweaters

The old me

The old me was better

But now I stay up late thinking about

How I ran out of thoughts

How I'm no longer a trend-setter

'Cause the old me

the old me

the old me was better

Leaving Life Lonely

Leaving life lonely

Laying in loss and lonesome

Lacking those luscious and lovely memories

Letting hate talk when I long to love

And to learn to be loyal

Leaning on the memories that are left

Lasting my final lungful of air

While leaving life lonely

MA

MA

my stability is off balance that it balances itself with the what's wrong

and what's not so wrong

look what i've done with my brain

MA

i deceived myself

tricked me into trusting wrong

when you were right

MA

i broke your heart

now you're flooding my soul

with your tears

MA

i lost my train of thought

hoping your train will track them

wake up

MA

13 Ways of Looking at a Picture

I.

Memories

Making way back to mind

Mastering other thoughts

Battling for old times

II.

Bring the dead back to life

Film holding back the urge

To go back in time

Days that will never again be mine

III.

A reminder of what used to be

Times where all mistakes weren't made by me

Moments when we

Where actually a family

IV.

Trying so hard to be her again

I liked it better when we were friends

I treat her so badly now
I don't when to go back or how

V.
Man and women
Were one
But now some papers
And missing rings
makes them done

VI.
The beauty and amusement
Roamed in the air
But now
I can't find it anywhere

VII.
Together we flew
when no one acted new
then we fell
we were threw

VIII.
The feather floated
We all blew to keep it up

The feather now
Has no luck

IX.
Crying together
Laughing together
Leaving the memories to die together

X.
A refresh to the mind
When everyone was so blind
To see what the future's going to do
No one ever listens to the truth

XI.
It was a rode to forever
Being alone
Never
Then I turned
I headed straight to the trap
Not knowing I was bait

XII.
Black and white
no color in sight

trying with all my might
to bring the dark some light

XIII.
Those "yeah I remember that"
And the "but we cant get it back"
"but what if we tried"
"naaw those days been died"

Mariah Cooper

The Eye of the Beholder

Written with Regan Nesbit

Blinded by the person they can only see
Beauty only comes with real personality
Made deaf by the compliments on just my looks
While I didn't take the time to realize what true beauty took
I don't know who I am only who I'm trying to be
Somebody who is not at all like me
But I'm supposed to please the people, right?
It's not like they can see the truth
Bumping right into the obvious clues
Because that girl lurking inside me
Doesn't like me or the person I'm trying to be
If only beauty wasn't a challenge I faced
Because the beauty I see is based on looks, body; race
You know if I was just a little lighter--maybe
They'd see my personality shines brighter--maybe
If my hair was less kinky
They would see that my hair doesn't define me
And if I didn't get such off-handed looks in so many places
Maybe people would see that I really could go places

They say beauty is in the eye of the beholder

Maybe I've given mine the cold shoulder

Maybe I can slide as perfect

But when they see me

I'm not worth it

All this time, effort that I put into looks

But they threaten my personality, creeping like crooks

Maybe if the world's attention was not wrapped up in blonde hair and blue eyes

You'd see that true beauty is where the soul lies

Because the look I have is more diverse

One of a kind in this universe

My skin should not land me in the pent house or the big house

Or inspire silence as quiet as a mouse

If you could see past a stereotype

You'd see my beauty is a rare type

I don't know the true definition of beauty

But I know where it starts

--With you

Because at the end you know

Who is truly beautiful

Mariah Cooper

Happy Ended

I remember riding my bike with my dad

Getting three layers on my ice cream

Going to the movies with my friends

Getting some cute little Converse

The good days

The ones everybody talks about

But what about when I fell off my bike

Or when my ice cream melted

What do I do when the movies ends

Or worst

Those cute little Converse don't fit no more

Nobody talks about then

Everybody just talks about the happy ending

Obviously there was no happy ending

But being happy did end.

Slave

slave to the rhythm

only his heart plays

mesmerizing aroma

when he walks it stays

warrior of love with faith as his shield

hoping he'll realize the hope i feel

wait where'd he go

did he leave

is he tired of me

or maybe he was imaginary

From the Back of My Closet

I am from the back of my closet

Sitting alone

Wishing for a diary and a locket

Always interrupted by "get your black crack down here"

Praying I won't hear

The laughter downstairs

Knowing I am up here

The pillow isn't soft enough

The trampoline doesn't bounce

The pool looks fun but no one will take me down

I am from the back of my closet where no one is around

A Poet

has my diction been misplaced

not qualified

good

but not heart-wrenching

dreams of manifested creativity strangle my nightmares

your pity aimed for my heart

the sun rusts over

before it missed

not a big fan of musicals

but are people born poets or is poetry thrust upon them

my pen the key to open the door to me

the agony of not picking the lock

and opening the door myself

accusing your words of hazing my soul

envy oozes down my spine

to my arm

being pumped into my brain

do i have the mind to finish this poem

the effort put into this pathetic poem

is unreal

Burial Ground

Rebirth for the death

Lost souls are not left behind

Start of an ending

**Mariah** is a thirteen year old girl with two brothers and three sisters. Mariah attends The Ron Clark Academy in Atlanta. Her inspiration came from her sixth grade English teacher Mrs. Barnes. Mrs. Barnes helped Mariah realize her love for writing and her gift for word. Mariah currently lives in Ellenwood, GA where she is busy at work creating new pieces for her next project.

Photo credit: J. Amezqua

Empowering young writers to say, **"I am my scholarship!"**

Open call for submissions to the *Young Writers Anthology*!

See your work in print!

    Become a published writer!

        **Earn royalites that can help
you pay for college!s**

VerbalEyze Press is accepting submissions from young adult writers, ages 13 to 22, in any of the following genres:

- poetry
- short story
- songwriting
- playwriting
- graphic novel
- creative non-fiction

For submission details, visit
www.verbaleyze.org

VerbalEyze serves to foster, promote and support the development and professional growth of emerging young writers.

VerbalEyze is a nonprofit organization whose mission is to foster, promote and support the development and professional growth of emerging young writers.

The *Young Writers Anthology* is published as a service of VerbalEyze in furtherance of its goal to provide young writers with access to publishing opportunities that they otherwise would not have.

Fifty percent of the proceeds received from the sale of the *Young Writers Anthology* are paid to the authors in the form of scholarships to help them advance in their post-secondary education.

For more information about VerbalEyze and how you can become involved in its work with young writers, visit www.verbaleyze.org.

www.ingramcontent.com/pod-product-compliance
Lightning Source LLC
Chambersburg PA
CBHW032104040426
42449CB00007B/1180